Mushrooms of the Grave

Written by Carl E. Miller and Lily Jo White

BOWMAN
CEMETERY
COURTESY OF ELKRUN TOWNSHIP TOURISM BUREAU

Introduction:

If you're an avid wild mushroom hunter or an enthusiast, then I'm sure you've searched long and hard for strange mushrooms throughout state parks and forests. However sometimes mushrooms can have a mind of their own, seemingly possessing the capabilities to appear just about anywhere— and if you take a trip to an old cemetery near you, then you might even see fungi growing there. Yet oddly enough they don't seem to only grow in cemeteries, but thrive in this setting.

Mushrooms growing in graveyards is hardly breaking news, with numerous reports of amateur hunters seeking these places out for several years. But why the mushrooms are growing there, is a topic that is rarely ever discussed. So I conducted my own research while I was working on a separate book titled, Wild Mushrooms of Ohio and Northern

Appalachia— and the results of this study are shocking!

When looking at an older graveyard, many things immediately stand out as to why mushrooms would enjoy this habitat, such as; plenty of shade, disturbed ground, moist environment, oftentimes partially, or completely, surrounded by woods etc. But an even deeper look will prove that it's perhaps even more complex than that. Several factors play a role in this strange phenomenon of graveyard mushrooms, so let's examine the evidence. But before continuing, please be respectful in any graveyard that you may find yourself in, and I advise you not to pick any of the mushrooms— but merely admire their uniqueness.

Graveyard moss:

Graveyard moss:

Flora such as; Sedum sarmentosum, Cypress spurge and others, are types of perennial ground covers and usually grow best in temperate regions. This flora is typically referred to as "graveyard moss" because it was, and still is, commonly planted in graveyards. Many mushrooms are ectomycorrhizal—meaning they have a symbiotic (Ectomycorrhizas) — give and take relationship with certain plants.

This relationship is possible by the fungi mycelium network attaching to the root system of specific trees and plants—Ectomycorrhizas only forms on the root system of around 2% of plants, roughly. With that being said, graveyard moss seems to serve as a magnificent host plant to numerous different types of wild mushrooms.

Mushrooms growing directly on, or near graveyard moss:

Vinca minor:

Vinca minor:

This plant is native to Europe, yet it can now be found in many temperate regions worldwide— due to its previous frequent use in graveyards. In the United States it was primarily used in graveyards that were in the Southern states, and less frequently used in Northern states. The older the graveyard, the better chances of you seeing this plant. If the graveyard has a wooded perimeter, and also has this flora, then expect the plant to have spread like a wildfire— it is an invasive species after all. Vinca minor is also used by many gardeners due to its low maintenance qualities, along with the plants Spring and Summer flowers.

If you happen to find this plant growing in the wild in the United States, there is a good chance you could be in a graveyard that no longer has any markers. But if you do stumble on this plant, and if the weather conditions are favorable, then you will likely find Chanterelle mushrooms— tons of them. These mushrooms grow plentiful, and Vinca minor seems to be an amazing host plant for Chanterelles, and likely plenty of other species of mushrooms such as the much sought after morels.

Vinca minor appears to be a special host plant because it forms a very dense sort of forest flora carpet, while also excluding nearly all other plants in the general area (essentially, by way of smothering). Although the plant's seemingly never-ending root system may be quite harmful for other nearby plants, they appear to be a dream come true for fungi mycelium networks to connect with.

Chanterelles forming a symbiotic relationship (Mycorrhiza) with Vinca Minor:

Gravestone:

Marble, granite and several other types of rock absorb and release water— which then creates both humidity and fog. Mushrooms are 90% water, so they crave these types of conditions. This is exactly why you shouldn't be too shocked the next visit you take to a local graveyard, and find mushrooms growing all around the gravestones— sometimes they even find a way through very tiny cracks in the stone itself.

These mushrooms need water in order to grow, and will always seek water out when necessary. This is exactly why they will even grow through the likes of stone in a graveyard, or perhaps even stone in your own backyard. Nothing is off limits with fungi, or so it seems at least. Always pay close attention when observing fungi, and understand that mushrooms are truly special, and they will be around long after humans are all gone.

Mushrooms growing around stone:

Dead Man's Fingers:

These Dead Man's Fingers (Xylaria polymorpha) mushrooms were found growing at the base of an injured tree along the trail to the haunted graveyard, adding even more mystique to the area. These mushrooms found in the forest can be odd enough, but when you spot them less than 100 yards away from a supposedly haunted graveyard, it seems very odd, to say the least.

These mushrooms were given the nickname Dead Man's Fingers, because oftentimes that is exactly what they look like when they are found growing— especially when they grow in small clusters like they usually tend to do.

Deformed Mushroom:

This deformed mushroom was found growing about 50 yards from the graveyard proper, right on the edge of the woods and likely attacked by the Bolete Eater fungus. The haunted history of Bowman's Cemetery dates a long ways back, and rumor has it that a witch is buried in these woods. The witch reportedly gave medicine to many sick children in the community, but when the childrens' health (shortly after her care) took a turn for the worse, she endured much of the blame.

The legend has it that the local townspeople gathered to hunt the witch down, and when they finally did they brought her back to the cemetery to be hanged. With many of the sick children buried in the cemetery, the locals wanted her to hang high from a nearby tree— so that she could look down at what she had done. They also insisted that her body be buried in the woods, rather than in the cemetery near the kids.

That witch is who supposedly haunts the nearby woods, with plenty of ghost-hunters and paranormal seekers claiming as much. There are several YouTube videos and articles written about the graveyards' purported haunted past, as well as numerous online reviews of varying peoples visits to the cemetery, where some claim things such as; having a strong feeling of being watched, or having things thrown at them. There are also reports of a crazed person who attacks your vehicle if you park nearby at night.

Mushrooms and graveyards both have a great amount of mystique, which typically leads to much imagination when either are being discussed in a film, or on television. Both can be looked at in a positive or negative light. For example, some people dismiss mushrooms altogether because they've heard of the potential of mushrooms being poisonous. I found this to be especially true when I personally conducted a study where I asked people that I knew what percentage of mushrooms they believed to be poisonous.

The majority of people that I surveyed said they believed half of mushrooms were poisonous. This was a surprise to me, but it shouldn't have been. So they've basically gone their entire lives fearing most mushrooms, when in reality, roughly only 3% are poisonous. However some of these poisonous mushrooms can be extremely deadly, which is what has sabotaged many peoples opinion when discussing fungi.

Graveyards aren't much different in that regard, these cemeteries are oftentimes considered haunted or creepy by some, and called a beautiful resting place by others. If you ask two people what their opinions are on graveyards, you're likely to get two totally different answers. According to "Little Witch Academia Wiki" fandom page, the television series Blytonbury's Undead Travelogue depicts a character being brought back to life using "Grave Mushrooms", along with some sort of weird spell. The mushrooms are described as being "red", "magical" and "only grow in graveyards". The mushrooms are also used to "call the souls of the dead", and also oddly described as possibly being poisonous.

Fowler's toad:

This Fowler's toad sitting on a grave in a supposedly haunted graveyard in Ohio, this toad uses defensive coloration to blend into its surroundings, making it a strange sight on a tombstone. This toad also burrows into the ground during hot days. Much like cemeteries, toads too are greatly associated with mushrooms— after all, poisonous ones are known as "toadstools".

This name is said to be given to poisonous mushrooms because in ancient times if a toad sat on a mushroom, they believed it to be poisonous, due to a large amount of toads being poisonous. However, roughly only 3% of mushrooms are poisonous— and there are more than 14,000 different types of mushrooms in the world. According to scientists, these mushrooms likely evolved on Earth more than 700 million years ago, yet they still somehow manage to amaze.

Some groups of fungi, more specifically the ammonia fungi and the postputrefaction fungi, have been long documented to be closely associated with the decomposition of cadavers. These mushrooms can be found throughout wooded areas and open fields across most of the world, sometimes even marking sites of graves— with some scientists even recommending that these mushrooms could serve as a tool for crime scene investigations.

Whether or not fungi can actually help crime investigations is still yet to be proven, but mushrooms are extremely complex— there is no debate at all about that. Some theorists, such as psychonaut philosopher Terrence McKenna, have even floated the idea that mushrooms may be a form of alien life.

To make things even stranger, there are even mushroom burial suits available, instead of a classic burial in a casket or cremation. These suits are made up of clothing with mushroom spores sewn into the fabric— and a big selling point is they are extremely environmentally friendly compared to traditional burial. The suit basically works by the mushroom spores colonizing the dead body, quickly decomposing it along the way.

However odd it may seem when you find a mushroom growing in a graveyard, there is a weird feeling that they also belong there. There aren't many things in life more mysterious and strange than a very old graveyard, and the same can also be said about mushrooms. So, naturally, when these two mysterious forces meet, the conditions can feel almost supernatural. This can be especially true if you go on a foggy Fall day, and if the graveyard happens to be purportedly haunted— well then that's just a bonus!

A cemetery that is not maintained very well is going to be your best bet for finding graveyard mushrooms, and the more remote the better. You should seek out any rural cemeteries for your adventure, but urban cemeteries may surprise you as well. Fungi growth can be an incredible thing to witness up-close, and the more you observe the more you will learn.

The graveyard that is referenced in this book (Bowman Cemetery) sits on half an acre of land and has graves that date back to the early 1800's, and the surrounding property is an abandoned coal mine. The mine was set-up by the Ferris Coal Company on a 1.7 acre property that was previously foreclosed in 1900. The coal mine operated there until 1988, when an investigation into the permits led to the site being abandoned altogether. However the effects can still be observed over 30 years later, especially when you look at the nearby creeks and streams and see the orange slime.

This coal mining waste (aka coal mine refuse) may also play a factor in this unusual mushroom growth in this area. Mushrooms have been used for toxic spills for their absorbent properties, however fungi can also benefit from toxic materials too. Mushrooms have a natural ability to use enzymes to break down foreign and toxic substances—essentially cleaning the surrounding environment while also benefiting. This process is known as Mycoremediation. Mycoremediation can have many other benefits as well, from the capabilities of using fungi to decontaminate the environment to improving surrounding soil.

Oddly enough, although mushrooms are oftentimes associated with death (due to some species preferring dead stuff to grow on) they can also be associated with immortality; such as how they were viewed in ancient Egypt. In Egypt during ancient times, only those who belonged to a royal family were allowed to consume them— since those in the royal family were thought to be descendants of Egyptian Gods. However Egypt wasn't the only country to associate mushrooms with longevity, both China and Japan share similar views.

Mushrooms also have a long history with witchcraft, with some historians stating that hallucinogenic mushrooms played a large role in witchcraft in Europe— namely the Amanita muscaria mushrooms.These mushrooms were believed to give these witches powers to fly, transform into different species, time travel and more. A very similar scenario occurred in the United States as well, when the fungus ergotamine (which grows on rye and barley) was cited as one of the main factors in the witchcraft phenomenon in Salem, Massachusetts.

The ergotamine fungus is also one of the main ingredients in LSD-25, an invention and discovery made by Swiss chemist Albert Hofmann. Hoffmann and his coworkers are also cited as isolating psilocybin as the primary cause for hallucinogenic effects in psilocybe mushrooms. Although I usually dislike the term "magic mushrooms" that is frequently used today, and rarely use the phrase myself, there is no denying that some, if not all mushrooms do in fact possess magical potentials— and not just the psilocybin ones. Keep in mind that all edible mushrooms contain some medicinals properties as well.

If you find the contents in this book interesting, then I strongly urge you to check out this phenomenon of graveyard mushrooms in person, and I also truly hope that you have enjoyed this book as much as I've enjoyed working on it! And once again, please be mindful of the graveyards you may find yourself in, remember that it is a resting place for people's loved ones—act accordingly and perhaps the mushroom Gods may bless you! **The End**